FREQUENTLY ASKED QUESTIONS ABOUT

Teen Fatherhood

Richard Worth

New York

Published in 2010 by The Rosen Publishing Group, Inc.
29 East 21st Street, New York, NY 10010

Copyright © 2010 by The Rosen Publishing Group, Inc.

First Edition

All rights reserved. No part of this book may be reproduced in any form without permission in writing from the publisher, except by a reviewer.

Library of Congress Cataloging-in-Publication Data

Worth, Richard.
Frequently asked questions about teen fatherhood / Richard Worth.—1st ed.
p. cm.—(FAQ: teen life)
Includes bibliographical references and index.
ISBN-13: 978-1-4358-5325-6 (library binding)
1. Teenage fathers—United States. 2. Teenage fathers—United States—Psychology. 3. Teenage parents—United States—Psychology. I. Title.
HQ756.7.W67 2010
306.874'2208350973—dc22

2008051938

Manufactured in the United States of America

R0432625408

Contents

Chapter one

WHO ARE TEENAGE FATHERS?

Most discussions of teen pregnancy focus on young women who become pregnant. There are more and more of them in the United States each year. But, of course, teen fathers also play an important role in the entire pregnancy process, as well as in the long-term responsibilities of raising a child. Unfortunately, teen fathers are frequently overlooked.

If you are a teen father, you're probably grappling with many conflicting feelings. Perhaps your first impulse was to regard the pregnancy as simply a bad dream that would go away when you woke up. When it didn't go away, you probably started asking yourself what you should do now that your partner is pregnant. Adolescence is usually not a time when anyone is thinking about becoming a parent. But here you are, along with your partner, confronting the reality of having a child.

Both mother and father play key roles in raising a child. Working together, they share responsibilities and help each other make important decisions.

While women play the key role in pregnancy, their partners also have a critical part to play in providing emotional support. There are important decisions that must be made together—not by the young woman alone. What's the best way to tell her parents and yours? How do you find a doctor who can provide your partner with proper medical care during her pregnancy? Other decisions include what kind of home to provide for your child, whether or not you'll need a part-time job to pay for

expenses, and how to complete your education. Some couples consider marriage, although the divorce rate is higher among teens than adults. Fortunately, those teens that make their marriage work are able to provide a warm and secure environment for their child. In the end, this is the most important thing.

After the child is born, your responsibilities as a father become even more essential. A child with an absentee father misses one of the most important people in his or her life. As a father, you provide a role model for your child. You serve as a teacher, a friend, and a loving companion—someone who is always there with a hug as your child walks along the road of life. Because you've become a teenage father, these will become part of your most unforgettable experiences. This book will answer some of the questions that you may have about fatherhood, and it will discuss ways to make fatherhood a fulfilling experience.

Teenage Fathers in the United States

If you are a teenage father, you're not alone. According to the Juvenile Justice Bulletin, between 2 and 7 percent of male teenagers in the United States become fathers each year. Anywhere from 900,000 to 1 million teenage girls become pregnant, and about one-third of those pregnancies are by teenage fathers.

The United States has the highest rate of teen pregnancy in the industrialized world. The rate had been declining for fifteen years. But, in 2005, it started to increase again by about 3 percent

Television star Jamie Lynn Spears and her teenage boyfriend, Casey Aldridge, became parents in June 2008.

annually. According to the March of Dimes organization, about one-third of all American girls now become pregnant before they turn twenty years old.

In 2008, one of these girls was seventeen-year-old Bristol Palin—daughter of Alaska governor Sarah Palin, the Republican nominee for U.S. vice president. Bristol's partner was eighteen-year-old Levi Johnston, also from Alaska. A year earlier, sixteen-year-old Jamie Lynn Spears, a star on the TV program *Zoey 101*, had announced she was pregnant. The father was her boyfriend, eighteen-year-old Casey Aldridge.

Sometimes, a relationship between a teenage girl and boy leads to pregnancy. Then, a couple must face important questions about their own future and the future of their child.

If you are a teenage father, you will probably never forget the experience of first learning that your girlfriend was pregnant. Perhaps she told you one day after school or during a break between classes. What were the words she used . . . the emotion in her voice . . . the expression on her face . . . as she gave you this news?

For any young girl, an entire range of feelings is likely to accompany her pregnancy. She may experience happiness over the idea of becoming a mother and having a baby to love. At Gloucester High School in Massachusetts, a group of eighteen girls got pregnant in one year. "They're so excited to finally have someone to love them unconditionally," one of their friends said. But other girls feel guilty about allowing themselves to become pregnant. Perhaps your partner tells you about the tremendous anxiety or fear that she feels over the way a baby will change her life. It will turn the rest of her teenage years into something quite different from what she expected. She might be fearful about telling her parents. And she might wonder if she is capable of handling all the demands of raising a child.

In interviews with *ABC News*, some teen girls who were pregnant talked about their feelings. One girl described herself as a "goody-two-shoes" who couldn't do anything because her mom, who worked in the school district, would find out. This girl was the captain of her golf team and was involved in her church. When she learned she was pregnant, she said, "This totally ruined my dreams." Later, she accepted the situation. Another girl added, "A lot of people are disappointed. They say, 'She's a waste,' and, 'Her whole future's going down the drain.'" It's not necessarily so.

Fatherhood Is a Process of Self-Discovery

Just as your girlfriend is experiencing a range of emotions, you, too, are dealing with your own reactions to the pregnancy. Your first reaction may be disbelief: "This can't be happening to me." You may ask your girlfriend whether she has been tested or if the test is accurate. If the answers are "yes," the realization sets in that she is pregnant. But you may still find yourself in a state of disbelief. "Wait," you say, "maybe I'm not the father. Maybe it was somebody else." From disbelief, you may move into a state of denial—refusing to believe that you are responsible for the pregnancy.

In most states, an unmarried couple is legally required to complete a form called an acknowledgment of paternity. This states the name of the father of the child so that he can be listed on the baby's birth certificate. If there is any question as to the identity of the father, it can be established by DNA testing from the tenth to twentieth week in a woman's pregnancy. Genetic material can be removed carefully by a doctor from a woman's uterus; it's the same as the genetic material from the fetus growing inside. This material is compared to a sample of the potential father's DNA. Using this method, paternity can be established with almost complete certainty.

If you are the father, a variety of feelings may rush through you. Some boys try to blame their girlfriends. They think that the girl should have been responsible and used some form of birth control to prevent the pregnancy. Clearly, however, birth

Often, a boy's reaction to the news of his girlfriend's pregnancy involves several stages. These may include disbelief, denial, blaming his partner, and finally, acceptance and taking responsibility.

control is a shared responsibility. Some teen fathers believe that their girlfriends wanted to become pregnant and have a child. This may be the case, but the fact is that most teenage pregnancies are unplanned. They "just happen" as two young people become involved in a highly charged, physical relationship.

From disbelief and denial, many teenage boys move to acceptance of their own responsibility in the pregnancy. For some, the overwhelming feeling is guilt for having caused the pregnancy. You may ask yourself, "Why did I allow this to happen?" It's easy to start blaming yourself. Throughout our lives, each of us is responsible for things that we wish afterward had never happened. It may be something we said that hurt another person's feelings, or something we did that fills us with regret. Unfortunately, there is no taking back of these things. They're done. We must live with our guilt and then move on. This is especially important if you become a teenage father. It's easy to let the feelings of guilt prevent you from dealing with the realities of the pregnancy. It's also easy to let your anxiety keep you from facing future decisions and responsibilities.

Feeling overwhelmed is a natural reaction when you must cope with a major change. Perhaps you have had to deal with the divorce of your parents, the death of a family member, or the experience of being forced to leave school and move to a different part of the country. These are significant changes that have a major impact on your life. They force you to adjust to new—and sometimes very painful—realities. Becoming a teen father is similar.

A teenage boy and girl who accept parenthood together have an opportunity to experience the joys of bringing a child into the world.

We're in This Together

As you start to deal with your changed life, try to remember that you are not alone. Things will not be exactly the same, but the people who cared about you before the big change still care about you now. Sometimes, you may feel cut off from your friends and different from everyone around you because you're trying to cope with something that they don't need to worry about. As the words of an old song put it, "Yesterday . . . all my

troubles seemed so far away." Now it's today, and the pregnancy has taken over your world and totally changed your life. But something else has changed, too—you and your partner are now joined together by a strong new bond.

You are not the only one who's adjusting to the pregnancy—there are two of you doing this together. As difficult as your feelings may be to deal with, your partner must cope with many of the same emotions—and more. If you are feeling alone and out of touch with your friends, remember that she is probably going through the same thing. What both of you share is very important, and so is the ability to communicate with each other as you move forward over the weeks and months ahead.

Males sometimes find that talking about their emotions is difficult. They don't want to appear weak or vulnerable. But all of your emotions, especially during a life-changing event like a pregnancy, are natural. It's also natural to express them to your partner. At the same time, it's not just about you. You need to think about her feelings. You need to empathize—put yourself in her place—and try to understand what she is experiencing. Both of you need each other's support.

There will be some intimate discussions that you and your partner will want to keep between the two of you. At the same time, don't be afraid to look for outside help. When you talk about the pregnancy with your partner, you may come up with more questions than answers. The experience is strange and foreign to you, but you are not the first young couple to go through it. So often, teenage couples try to hide a pregnancy because they feel guilty about it or they fear the reaction of

others. But counseling from a sympathetic, experienced adult can be extremely helpful. This may be a teacher, a doctor or other health professional, someone in your family, or a member of the clergy.

An adult can help you and your partner look ahead and begin the planning process that is so necessary now that you must make decisions about the pregnancy.

Chapter two

WHAT IS FATHERHOOD ALL ABOUT?

Choosing to become a father is a big decision—probably the most important one that you can ever make. Fatherhood has its joys and its challenges. There is the emotional gratification that comes from bringing a newborn into the world. There is also the overwhelming sense of responsibility to care for a helpless baby. One young father was surprised by how taking care of a baby involves "just basically everything." Some teens have grown up in single-parent families where their own fathers were absent. As one of them explained, he and his partner "want to break the cycle of not having a dad around."

Fatherhood enables you to experience the pleasure of giving yourself to someone else who is totally dependent on your love and caring. But don't overlook the day-to-day tasks that also come along with fatherhood. Babies need lots of attention. Whether or not that

While parenthood involves work, it also provides many satisfactions. Nurturing your child can give you a sense of fulfillment unlike any other experience in your life.

attention is necessary during the day or in the middle of the night, you or your partner must be there to tend to the needs of your child.

Alternatives to Becoming Your Child's Father

Some people decide to avoid the challenge of parenthood. Adoption, for example, is one of the options that some teenage couples choose. This is especially the case if they're not prepared to raise a child themselves. Adoption is relatively common: In the United States, there are approximately 1.5 million adopted children. States require both the mother's and father's consent to give up a child before adoption can occur. However, the father may lose this right if he has abandoned his partner or has refused to provide support for the mother and child.

Adoption has two main purposes. First, it aims to provide a stable, loving family for a child who might not have one otherwise. The other aim is to give children to people who cannot have them. For many teen fathers and mothers, adoption is a way to make a good situation out of a bad one.

The decision to give up a baby for adoption requires serious consideration. By giving up your child, you may feel a great sense of loss and sadness. Some parents feel guilty after placing their child up for adoption, and the guilt may never disappear. You may never stop thinking about your child or wondering what might have happened if you and your partner had decided to raise the child yourselves.

Approximately one-third of all teen pregnancies end in abortion. In the United States, abortions generally occur in the first trimester, or the first three months of pregnancy. Some teenagers wait beyond the first trimester, largely because they are afraid to tell their parents about the pregnancy. But a majority of states ban late-term abortions. Some states also require that one parent give permission before a female under the age of eighteen can have an abortion. Others require that one or both parents must be told, although their permission is not necessary.

Raising Your Child

In his article "Adolescent Pregnancy: Current Trends and Issues," Jonathan Klein noted that more than half of all teenagers who become pregnant give birth. Many decide to raise their children. While some become single parents, others share the parenting role with their male partners. Rarely does a single factor drive their decision. There may be a strong bond and deep affection between the two parents. Some may feel a sense of joint responsibility to the child. Others may have a strong desire to take on parenting roles.

Even if you feel all of these things, you should also be aware of the challenges that await teen parents. Perhaps the first of these is the conversation that a teen couple must have with their parents or guardians. It's important for you and your partner to talk with your parents about many of the issues confronting you both. How will you balance the demands of parenting with the

Some very difficult conversations will involve what you say to your parents and hers about raising your child.

need to finish your education? How are you going to provide financial support for your child? How will parenthood affect the amount of time that you can spend enjoying activities with your family and friends? Gather all the information you can. Talk to other adults whose opinions you value, e-mail friends who have faced the same decision that is confronting you, log on to Internet Web sites, and read materials from the library. Then, when the time is right, sit with your parents and discuss these and other issues together.

Talking to your and your partner's parents provides a clear indication that both of you have carefully thought through your decision. Parents generally react with surprise and shock when they first hear the news about a pregnancy. They may offer you their support or disagree with your choice to begin a new family. Some girls' parents are so opposed to the pregnancy that the fathers just walk away from the situation. Don't make that mistake. Support your partner, discuss your decision calmly, and give her parents time to adjust to what lies ahead. This is only one of many challenging situations that you will face as a teen father. While it may be easy to give up, everyone involved is going to be better off if you make the commitment to being the best father that you can be.

Myths and Facts

Teenage fathers abandon their partners.

Fact → Many teen fathers remain involved with their partners. This does not necessarily mean that the couple marries. Frequently, they do not enter marriage, but most stay involved with each other.

Teenage fathers are financially irresponsible.

Fact → Naturally, most teenage fathers want to provide financial support for their partners and their children. However, they often are incapable of finding a job that will enable them to carry out their financial responsibilities. They may also be unable to balance working and going to high school. State laws, however, require a teen father to provide money for raising his child.

VINTAGE MODERN

THOMAS O'BRIEN

Teenage fathers abandon their children.

Fact → Historically, teen fathers often stay involved with their children. One 1993 report on a study by the Teen Fatherhood Collaboration found that a majority of teen fathers "saw the children frequently" and provided part of their care. This included bathing, feeding, and emotional support. A *Time* magazine article from 2005 confirms the trend. According to the article, after a two-year study of four hundred teenage fathers, the Bank Street College of Education in New York City found that more than 80 percent had contact with their children every day. And more than 90 percent continued to have a relationship with the mother of their child.

Chapter three

HOW DO YOU PREPARE FOR THE BIRTH OF YOUR CHILD?

There are many things that you will need during the early days of pregnancy. Among the most important is empathy for your partner, or the ability to put yourself in her place and understand what is happening to her. In order to nurture the baby that's growing inside her, your partner's body is producing larger amounts of hormones. These chemicals often cause significant mood swings. At one moment, she may feel excitement about her pregnancy, followed by anxiety over becoming a parent. In addition, during the first trimester, many women experience morning sickness, which is nausea and vomiting that occur after they eat, usually in the morning. In the first trimester, your partner may also feel exhausted much of the time and have difficulty sleeping.

Before the birth, during what is called the prenatal period, proper health care is essential for a pregnant

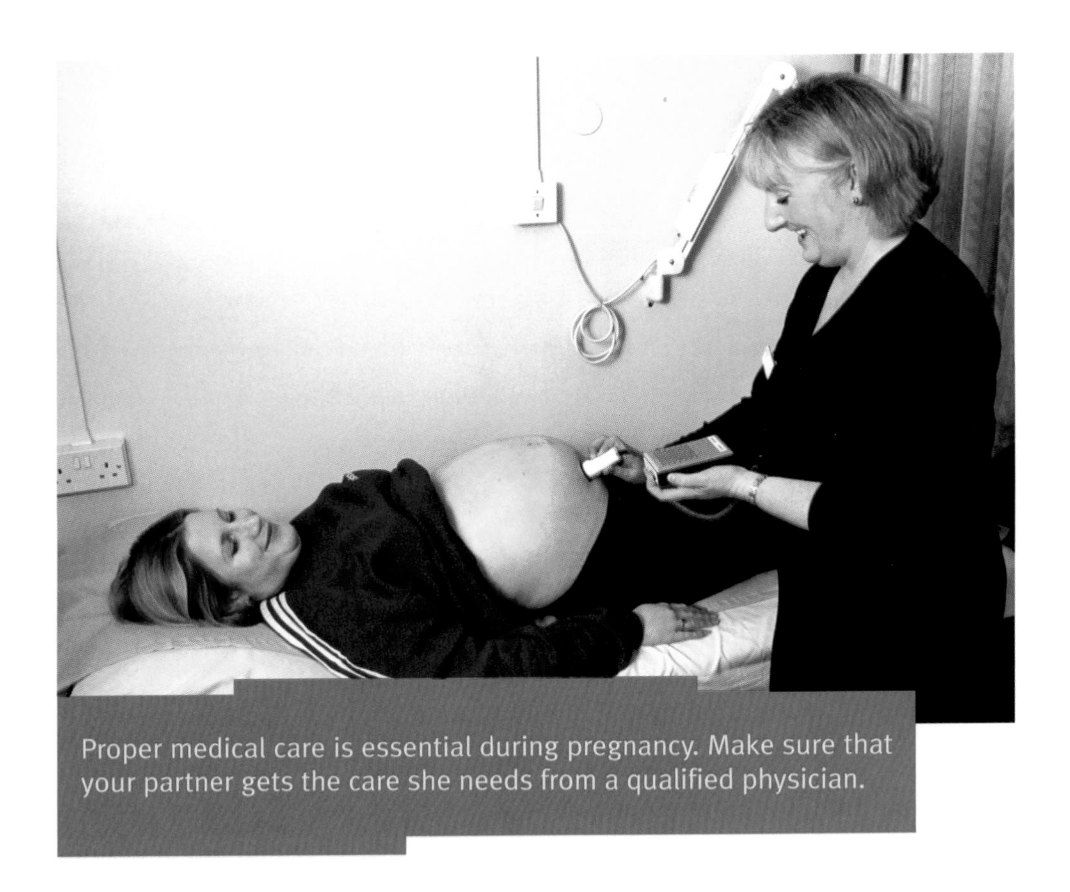

Proper medical care is essential during pregnancy. Make sure that your partner gets the care she needs from a qualified physician.

woman. Some teenage girls are afraid to admit that they are pregnant. So, they fail to consult a physician or go to a health clinic during the first trimester. Others try to hide their pregnancy from parents or friends because they feel ashamed that it happened. They may never visit a gynecologist/obstetrician during their pregnancy. It is up to you and your partner to make sure that she receives good prenatal care. If your partner's parents have health insurance, it is likely to cover prenatal care as well as the baby's delivery.

More than older women, teenage girls are at risk for high blood pressure during pregnancy. They are also more at risk for anemia, which is a lack of red blood cells that can lead to physical weakness. Mothers-to-be need to take special vitamins during pregnancy and eat regular meals. But studies show that teenagers often do not eat properly and gain enough weight during their pregnancy. As a result, their children may be underweight at birth. Today's medical treatment for low-birth-weight babies—under 5.5 pounds (2.5 kilograms)—is very successful, so low birth weight alone is rarely life threatening. However, babies born underweight may have underdeveloped organs, difficulty breathing, poor vision, and other problems. Also, the death rate among these low-birth-weight babies is higher than among other babies.

While proper nutrition during pregnancy is essential to the health of a newborn, a woman must also take other precautions. Smoking cigarettes and drinking alcohol have a negative impact on the growth of a fetus and can cause birth defects. All prescription and over-the-counter drugs should be avoided as well, unless they are prescribed by a physician who knows that the young mother is pregnant.

As a father-to-be, you need to safeguard your own health. Remember to stay in good physical shape. Exercise, eat well, and get plenty of rest. You will need to be physically and mentally sharp to deal with all the demands of your partner's pregnancy, the birth, and the responsibilities of fatherhood. Avoid alcohol and recreational drugs, which will only complicate your life at this time.

Birthing Classes

During the third trimester, many prospective parents participate in birthing classes. This experience will strengthen the bond between you and your partner in preparation for the arrival of your child. In these classes, you will meet other people who are expecting children. This will give you a chance to share your experiences during the pregnancy and to acquire additional information in preparation for the birth.

Many birthing classes use the Lamaze technique. This technique teaches a woman how to relax during delivery, breathe properly, and deal with the pain of childbirth. Other classes teach the Bradley method, which involves the father as a woman's birth coach during the delivery. Classes are available at hospitals, community health clinics, and from privately run programs. Ask your physician to recommend a class.

A Home for Your Child

As the delivery day gets closer, you and your partner must deal with the details of providing a home for the child. If your mate has maintained a close relationship with her parents, she may prefer to stay in her own home and raise the child there. In some cases, her mother and father may even be looking forward to becoming grandparents and will be happy to lend a hand with child care. As you consider this alternative, however, make sure that her parents will also welcome you into their home and make you feel comfortable there. One way to create

It's important to work together with your partner to provide a comfortable room for the baby. This may be located at her parents' home, your parents' home, or at your own apartment.

a good relationship with the future grandparents is to visit them as much as possible. Assure them that you are planning to support their daughter and carry out all of your responsibilities as a father. This will make it easier for you to play your necessary role in raising your child.

In some cases, the best place to raise a child may be in your home. Perhaps your mother and father have accepted the pregnancy more easily than your partner's parents have. Perhaps your mother or another relative in your home is in the best

position to be a caregiver to your baby. Maybe there is more space available to provide a nursery room for the child. The decision on where your baby lives will require discussions between you and your partner, as well as with both of your parents.

Some teenage couples consider establishing a separate home in an apartment. For most young couples, this option is too expensive. Generally, there are so many other expenses related to the child that making rent payments is unrealistic. In fact, paying for your child's things may require you and your partner to spend all your savings and even accept financial help from your parents.

A partial list of what your baby will need includes a bassinet or crib with sheets, a stroller, and an infant car seat for transporting the child safely in a vehicle. You'll also have to purchase a variety of other items, such as diapers, bodysuits, socks or booties, and hats for the baby to wear. Then, there are bibs, receiving blankets, and burp cloths, as well as towels, bathing soaps, baby wipes, a diaper pail, diaper rash ointment, baby powder, lotions, and other supplies to keep the baby clean. Don't forget about bottles, a bottle sterilizer, and baby formula for feeding time. You'll probably want or need pacifiers, a rocking chair, play mats, soft toys, mobiles, sound monitors, a changing table, a humidifier, a baby thermometer, a bulb syringe, and more!

Perhaps your parents kept some of these items—like a crib or stroller—that they used when they were raising you or your siblings. Ask to borrow them to avoid the cost of buying new ones. In addition, your partner's friends may decide to hold a

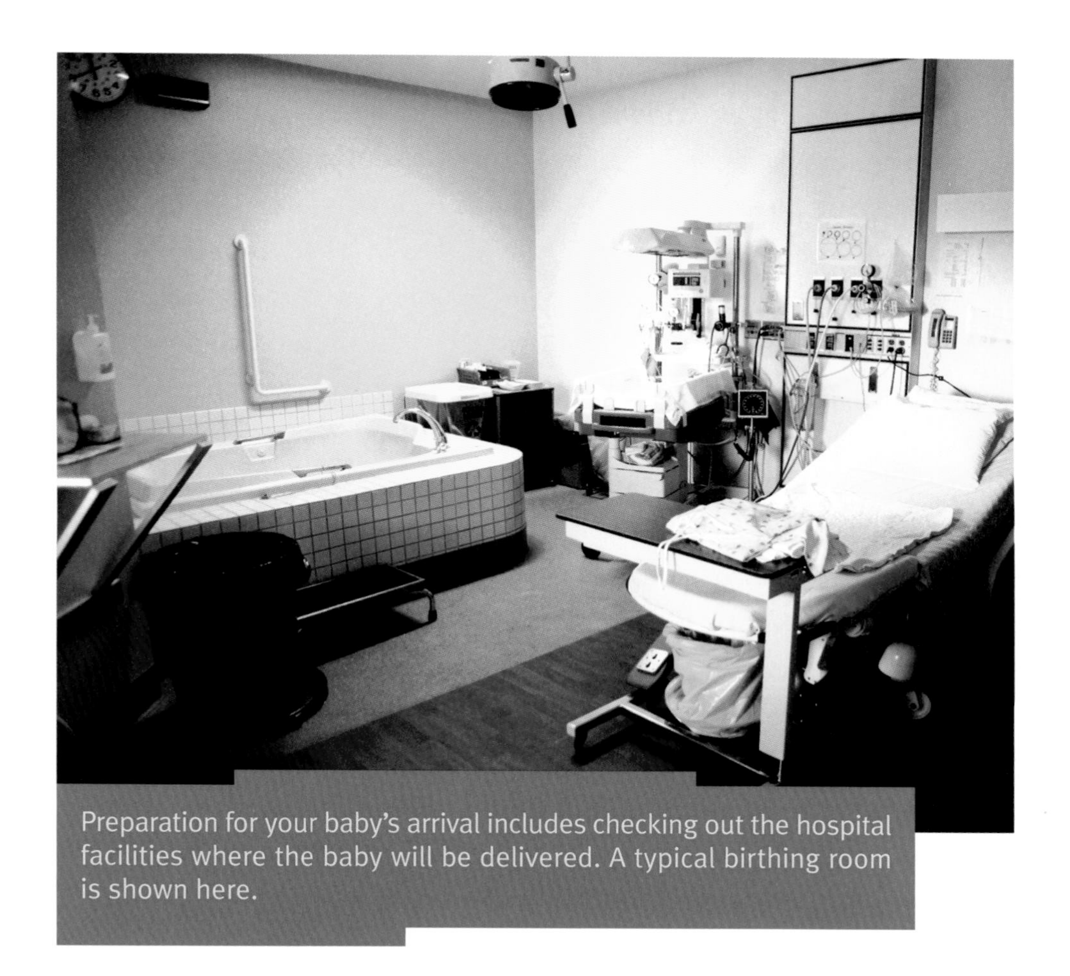

Preparation for your baby's arrival includes checking out the hospital facilities where the baby will be delivered. A typical birthing room is shown here.

baby shower for her. The gifts she receives at this event are items that she and the baby will need.

Day of Delivery

As the day of delivery approaches, you and your partner will experience the anxiety and the excitement that affect all

expecting couples. Share your feelings with each other. Reassure your mate, and make sure that she knows you will be supporting her throughout the entire birthing process. If you've participated in birthing classes, you'll want to play an important role in the delivery room. As her coach, you can provide emotional support and help her remember all the methods that she learned during the birthing class to make the delivery easier.

As the delivery date approaches, be sure to check out the hospital. Make sure that you know where it is located, where the delivery room is, and how to get there. Also make sure that it is clear who will take your partner to the hospital when she is due to deliver the baby. Remind your partner to prepare a bag with important items that she will need for her stay in the hospital. It is smart to do this far in advance of the due date, as it is not uncommon for babies to be born four or five weeks ahead of schedule.

Check out her parents' insurance, which probably covers her, and make sure that it has maternity benefits. These include such things as the doctor's fees for delivering the baby and the cost of the hospital room, as well as nursing care.

For some unfortunate teen fathers, your presence in the delivery room creates a problem for your partner's parents. They may blame you for the pregnancy and be unwilling to accept you as a full participant in the birth of your child. Don't be afraid to stand up for your right to be present when your partner delivers the baby. At the same time, be sensible and do what you can to avoid an unpleasant situation that can negatively affect your mate's delivery.

If all goes well, and you're there when your child is born, you'll experience the thrill of welcoming a new life into the world. This is also an important day for your partner, one that changes her life, too. And, of course, it's an event that must be shared with new grandparents. Whether their reactions are positive, negative, or somewhere in between, they are part of your new family—a group that will bring you joys, challenges, and responsibilities.

chapter four

HOW DO YOU FIND BALANCE IN YOUR LIFE?

As a teen father, you have a unique dual role. Unlike most of your peers, you are not the average adolescent. While your peers may focus much of their attention on sports, extracurricular activities, socializing, and schoolwork, you have another focus that is altogether different. You have taken on the responsibilities of both an adult and a father while you are still a teenager. In this dual role, you will confront many decisions that other teens do not face.

Making Decisions

Experts have developed a five-step process to help people make decisions. This process doesn't tell you what to choose, only how to smartly go about making the choices that lie ahead for you. Using this process gives

Decision making is a skill that you can look to improve all the time. Making good decisions now will have lasting effects on both you and your child.

you a sensible framework for making just about any big decision and can help you maintain a good balance in your new life.

Step One: Identify the decision that you need to make.
Sometimes, we just act without recognizing that there are alternatives we can explore. For example, a four-year college may seem like the only step to take after high school, until you begin to consider other options—two-year community college, trade school, military service, or a temporary job between high school and college. Don't act on the first idea that comes to your mind. Instead, take the time to explore your alternatives.

Step Two: List your options and collect information about them.
Brainstorm the different choices that you might make, and then learn more about each of them. This data gathering may take some time. You might need to consult adults who can give you advice based on their own experience. Often, the mistakes they made can help you avoid similar ones. Other sources of information could include the Internet and the books in your school or local library, as well as magazine and newspaper articles.

Step Three: Determine the pluses and minuses of each alternative.
What frequently makes decisions so difficult is that no option seems perfect—each one has its pros and cons. Research helps you figure out the positives and negatives for every option. Then, you can make two columns—pro and con—under each option, and list the positives and negatives. If you have unanswered

questions, go back and do more research. By looking at your two lists, you can determine which option has the most pluses and the fewest minuses. This is usually the best choice for you to make.

Step Four: Consider your values and feelings.

Hard facts are not the only factors that we take into consideration when we make decisions. We should also listen to our feelings and test each alternative against our values. There may be several good reasons for selecting a certain option. However, that option may go against one of your strongly held values. Therefore, you must reject it. On the other hand, your feelings may push you strongly in one direction. But after carefully examining all the evidence with a cool head, it can become clear that another option is a better choice.

Sometimes, feelings and values can conflict. Fear may take hold when you face a difficult challenge, and you may want to run away from it. But a strong sense of responsibility keeps you in there, confronting the challenge head-on.

Step Five: Choose the best option for you.

After listing the options, looking at the information about each one, and considering your feelings and values, you are ready to make a decision. The choice may still be a hard one, but at least you can tell yourself that you've done everything possible to go with the best option. This may not be the one that your friends or even your parents would choose. But if it is the best one for you, go for it.

Doing your schoolwork as you shoulder the responsibilities of parenthood will often seem exhausting, but the payoff will come in the future.

What Should I Do About School?

Let's use the decision-making framework to look at important decisions that you will face as a teen father. Don't forget that you have already made one very significant decision: to become a father and stay involved with your partner and your child. Some teenage boys let their feelings dictate their decision and run away from fatherhood, leaving the responsibility entirely up to their partner. You, on the other hand, have been guided by a strong set of values. You have accepted your role in the birth of your child, and you are staying committed to your relationship.

Another big decision is whether or not you should finish high school. Among the teen fathers involved in one study, only about 50 percent graduated from high school. Many of the teenagers in the study were already having problems in school.

As a father with a good job, you can derive satisfaction from your work and the knowledge that you are providing for your child.

They had lost interest and wanted to do something else with their lives. Their partner's pregnancy may have given them a reason to leave school and find a job. In part, they were driven by their negative feelings about school. They were also motivated by a sense of responsibility to their new family and a desire to support them financially. One of the young fathers said that he needed a job to fulfill his financial responsibilities to his new child. Another emphasized that he wanted to take care of his family by himself and not look to other people for financial help.

Yet, many of these boys recognized the importance of an education. They realized that without an education, doors in the workplace would be closed to them. Amy Williams, executive director of the Teenage Pregnancy and Parenting Project in San Francisco, California, pointed out that teens who drop out of high school "head right for a low-paying job." Another expert added, "Five years down the line, they won't have skills to qualify for much more than work in a fast-food restaurant."

A study of teen fathers in Connecticut confirmed this statement. It showed that teen fathers who leave high school may initially make more money than their peers who stay in school. But down the road, when these males have reached their mid-twenties, they usually earn far less than those who have received a high school education or have continued on to college.

The message is clear: Your feelings may be pushing you to quit school. But the facts show that an education is essential to being a good teenage father and supporting your family.

Public schools have responded to this message by establishing programs designed to help young fathers stay in school. There is the Teen Parent Program in Boulder, Colorado, for example. It helps teenage mothers and fathers complete their education while also providing a daycare program for their children. In this program, teen parents learn more than just the skills of parenting and child development. They also take academic courses necessary for high school graduation and receive career training and guidance. A similar program operates at New Futures School in Albuquerque,

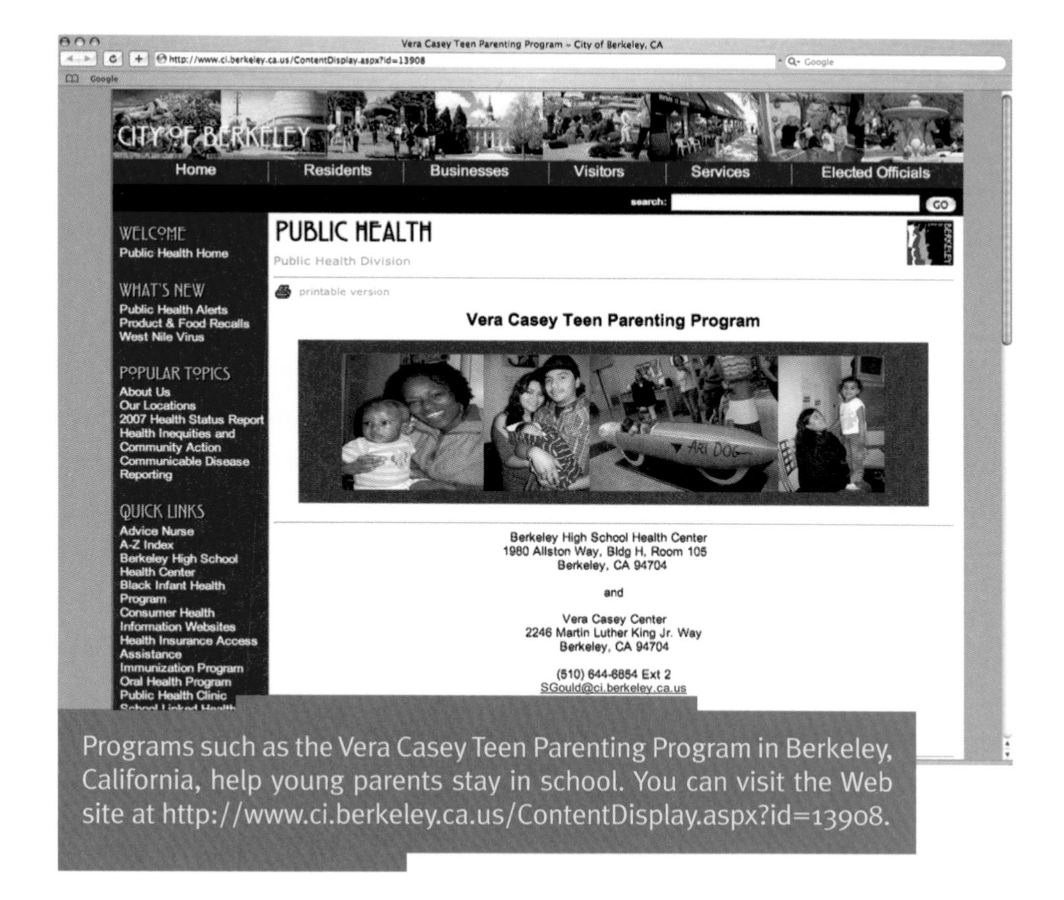

Programs such as the Vera Casey Teen Parenting Program in Berkeley, California, help young parents stay in school. You can visit the Web site at http://www.ci.berkeley.ca.us/ContentDisplay.aspx?id=13908.

New Mexico. Your school may also offer programs designed to help teenage fathers.

Gary Simmons advises teen fathers in Pennsylvania. His two primary goals are to keep these young men in school and ensure that they become responsible fathers. He emphasized that quitting school is not the answer to becoming good fathers, noting, "They're not going to provide very much as a high school dropout."

Should My Partner Stay in School?

It's important, too, for teenage mothers to try to stay in school while they raise their children. The March of Dimes is a charity dedicated to improving the lives of babies. According to one of their recent reports, approximately 40 percent of teen mothers complete high school and receive a diploma. The other 60 percent will not have the qualifications to obtain a job that can financially support them and their children. As a result, many of these women will live in poverty. Programs like New Futures and the Teen Parent Program serve both moms and dads. Indeed, there are usually far more girls enrolled in such programs than boys.

Similar programs have been started in the school districts of Gloucester, Massachusetts; Miami, Florida; Springfield, Missouri; and Marion County, Indiana. In the Marion County program, more than 90 percent of the participating seniors graduated from high school. Many schools also offer teen mothers the option of taking courses at home. While your partner is studying, you can help her out with child care or with any other task that she needs you to do. This will enable her to complete a high school education while still being a responsible mother.

Talk to administrators at your high school and find out if programs are available to help you and your partner balance education and parenting. These programs help teenage mothers and fathers receive the education and skills that they need to provide financially secure homes for their children.

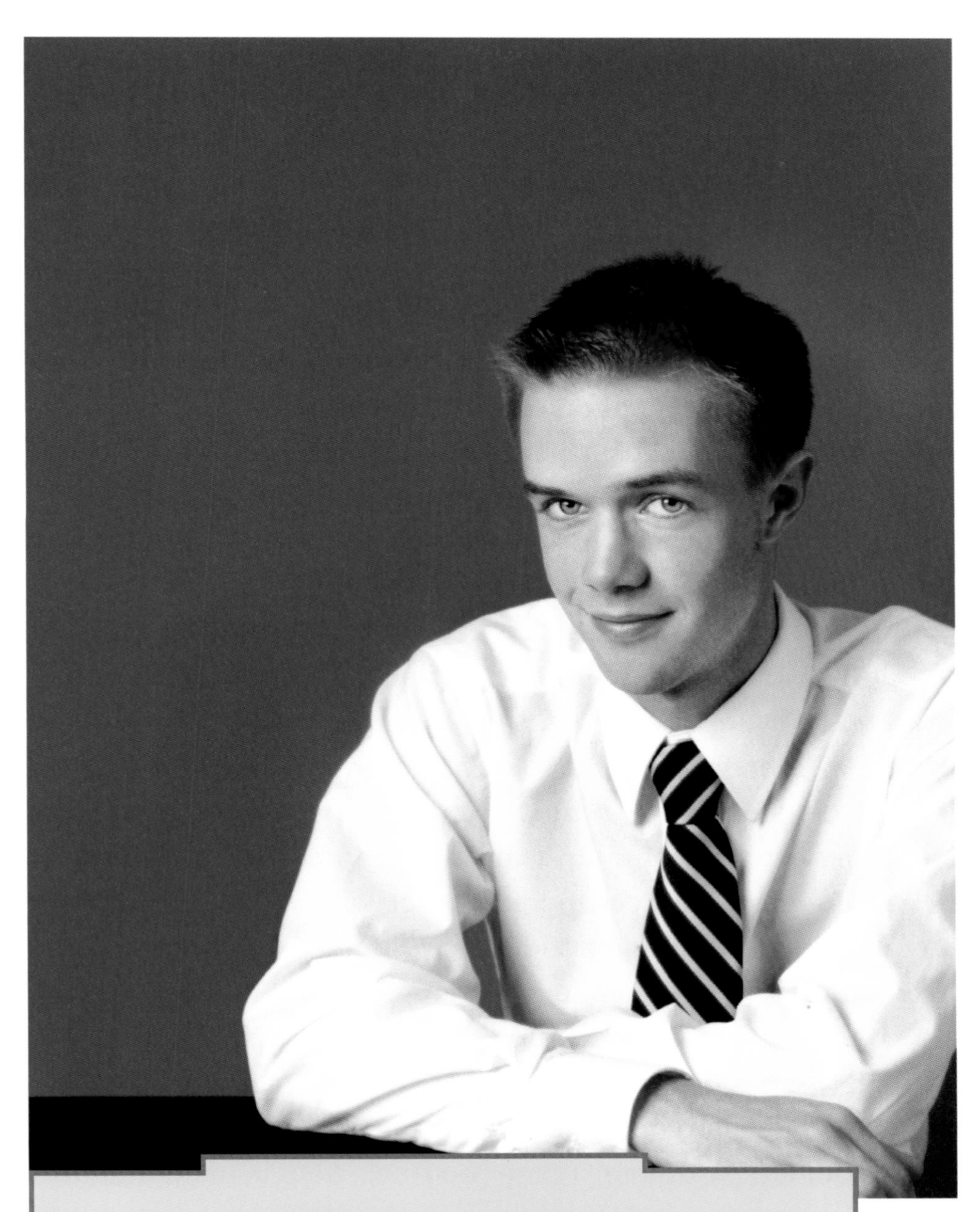

The experience of fatherhood can make you better at planning and balancing the many demands of adult life.

Should You Look for Part-Time Work?

When you made the decision to become a father, you also took on some of the financial responsibilities of raising your child. While your parents and your partner's parents may be willing to help you out financially, you still bear an obligation to support your new family. In fact, state laws require you to provide financial support for your child. These laws, called paternity laws, are designed to provide the child with some security. The laws permit states to take part of a father's wages if he is not fulfilling his obligations.

As you have already decided to become a father and stay involved with your family, you will want to do as much as possible to support them financially and in other ways. The risk is that you may try to do too much, work too many hours, and burn out trying to balance a job, school, and parenting. Here again, it's best to base your decision about working on facts as well as feelings.

The best way to begin is by making a daily schedule. Write down the hours that you spend in school, how much time you need to devote to homework, and which hours you are engaged in parenting your child. This will give you an idea of how much time is left for a part-time job.

Next, decide if there is any work that you are already experienced to do. Perhaps you once held a summer job at a nature center, so you're trained to do this kind of work. If you enjoyed this job, look for another position in the same field. It makes working that much easier.

If you have no previous job training, the best place to start is the employment section of the newspaper or online. There, you can find out who is hiring entry-level workers. Often, these are fast-food restaurants and retail stores in shopping malls. You might also try networking, or talking to friends and acquaintances to find out if they know of any employers who need part-time workers.

When applying for a job, the first step is to fill out an application. The next step is to telephone the employer and set up an interview. If you've never done this before, it can make you nervous. Everyone feels the same way. It's best to keep the conversation simple: Introduce yourself, and ask the employer when you could make an appointment. And make sure that it does not conflict with your classes.

When you appear for the interview, make sure that you arrive on time and are neatly dressed. This makes an excellent first impression. As you talk to the employer, show enthusiasm for the job. Employers want to hire energetic employees. Ask about the hours of employment and be sure that they fit with your schedule. Don't agree to work too many hours. You will feel exhausted at the end of your work shift, and you'll be unable to do your schoolwork and too tired to carry out your parenting responsibilities.

After you get the job, tell the employer that you are a father with a young child. Many employers feel that parents make more responsible employees. Good employers will try to be sensitive to a parent's needs and help you arrange a work schedule that enables you to care for your child.

Part-time jobs are usually low-paying jobs, so you'll need to be very careful with your money to ensure that it stretches as far as possible. Teen fathers have expenses for their children, as well as expenses for themselves. The only way to figure out these expenses is to make a weekly or monthly budget. This might include what you spend on items like clothing, food, toys, and child care for your baby. You may also include the cost of operating a car, as well as rent and utilities for an apartment.

Add up all of these expenses. Chances are that the weekly take-home pay from your job won't cover all of these expenses. Although your partner's main responsibility is to her child, she may also need to work part-time. You still may need to rely on help from parents in order to make ends meet.

The Future of Your Relationship

As teen parents wrestle with the challenges that confront them, many begin to think about the future of their relationship together. What form should that relationship take? What would be best for them and their child? A good way to gather the facts and make a decision is to talk to a counselor who is skilled in marriage and family relationships.

Ten Great Questions to Ask a Counselor

1. What are the success rates among teenage married couples?

2. How do we know if we're ready to settle down and marry?

3. How do we figure out our commitment to each other?

4. How will marriage affect our education and career plans?

5. How will marriage impact our chances to enjoy being teens?

Is living together and remaining unmarried a realistic alternative for us?

7

How will her parents/my parents react to our living together?

Should we live apart and care for our child?

9

If we live apart, how can I remain involved as a parent?

Will I still feel a commitment to my partner if we live apart?

chapter five

HOW DO WE BECOME SUCCESSFUL PARENTS?

With the birth of a baby, your priorities change. Now, you have far more than yourself to worry about. You have a family—your partner and your child. After childbirth, your partner may experience the "baby blues." This is a sadness or irritability caused by a sudden change in her hormone activity once the baby has been delivered. She may also have trouble sleeping, and the demanding task of caring for a baby without enough sleep can make your partner feel even more anxious. Generally, the blues last only a few days or weeks after the delivery. During that time, try to be as sensitive as you can to your partner's feelings. Also, suggest that she talk to family, friends, or other new mothers.

Unfortunately for some women, the baby blues can continue much longer than just a few days or weeks. In that case, the symptoms are called postpartum depression.

Child rearing is a shared responsibility for you and your partner. You'll care not only for the child but also for each other as you deal with the strong emotions that come with parenthood.

If this occurs, you should urge your partner to talk to a doctor who can help her deal with the depression.

Don't neglect your own feelings as you begin raising a child. You'll probably be experiencing ups and downs that change from day to day. On one hand, there is the joy of parenthood, watching a tiny infant who is totally dependent on others to tend to his or her every need. On the other hand, there is the awesome responsibility of providing the right kind of care so that your child can develop properly. Try to remember that people—no matter what their ages—usually have very little experience

As a parent, it's impossible to be prepared for every situation, and you'll need advice from time to time. If you don't know, don't be afraid to ask.

with parenting when they become parents for the first time. They must learn the ropes. You can learn them, too.

Communication and Advice

A key to successful parenting is good communication between mother and father. It's important that you and your partner decide what roles to fill in raising a child. If the child is living at your partner's home along with her parents, she may bear more of the responsibility than you do. She may be the one who gets

up when the child cries during the night. And she may handle most of the baby's feedings during the day. If she is attending a school that provides child care, the baby will have trained staff to provide a loving and secure environment for him or her during the day. If not, one of your partner's parents or your parents may have to help out with child care.

Some schools also offer programs that help young mothers adjust to their new roles and learn how to handle them well. As one program administrator put it, "We kind of just talk about issues they struggle with, have difficulty with, or just kind of laugh about the crazy things little kids do." The programs include parenting classes and an opportunity to share joys—and frustrations—with other teen parents.

As for your part, even before the child's birth, you should begin reading books about infant care and deciding what you can do to be a good father. Some teenagers have grown up in a single-parent family, where their fathers played little or no role in raising them. Better than anyone else, they know what it means to not have a father present at a young age. Fathers provide positive role models, especially for their sons. Indeed, statistics show that when fathers are not involved, their children are far more likely to leave high school without a diploma and experience emotional problems as adults.

There are times of the day when your partner may be in school or at a part-time job. That's when you can play the role of the main caregiver for your child. To provide good care, you should know how to bathe and feed a child, change diapers, and put the child to bed. Bath time is an excellent time to bond with

your baby, as you wash and dry him or her. Try singing to the baby in the bathtub or after the bath is over. "In teen mentality," said one expert who works with teen fathers, "it's not cool when you're down on the floor singing to a baby. We're trying to get them past that. It's the coolest thing you could possibly do."

Experiencing the Growth of Your Child

A child's growth happens very quickly. Every moment that you're not there is a moment when you may miss an extraordinary step in his or her development. Maybe your child grasps a new toy and coos with delight. The child looks in your face, and a broad smile suddenly appears across his or her face. The diaper needs to be changed and your baby cries in distress. He or she begins crawling across the floor. One day, your child takes that first, shaky step. These are the events that you want to experience as a new father. Of course, it's not always easy, especially if your child is living at your partner's home. But by making fatherhood a top priority in your life, you can schedule time to participate in raising your child.

Child rearing can also be frustrating. No two people are always going to agree on how to raise a child. For this reason, it's highly recommended that you and your partner take parenting classes. This is important for parents of all ages, but especially for teens. Parenting classes will help you understand your roles when it comes to caring for the baby and for each other. You'll learn how to discuss things together and compromise. This may mean you stay at home for the evening, even though you really

Little babies are not all smiles all the time. During the first few months, they can require your attention around the clock.

want to go out and leave the baby with a sitter. It may mean being flexible when your partner takes you shopping for baby clothes and selects something that might not be your first choice. It can also mean dealing with her parents, who may resent your presence in their home and blame you for what happened to their daughter. Remember that your role in child rearing is more important than what they might think of you. It's essential to stay involved, even if the going gets rough.

Babies require patience, especially when they become upset, push their food onto the floor, or throw a tantrum. Never shake

Dinnertime can be fun for a father and child. It can also be very challenging, especially when your child is reluctant to eat and wants to do something else.

or strike your baby. Try to remind yourself that they are only infants, and their actions are a normal part of their behavior. Take a deep breath and count to ten if you have to. Become a teacher—discipline your child gently, and show him or her what to do. Being a teacher is one of the most important roles that you can play for your child.

You're also a role model for the child. As he or she grows older, your child will observe how you treat your partner and others and will begin to understand what healthy relationships are all about. While some men are uncomfortable showing affection, never hesitate to hug your child, cuddle with your child, and demonstrate your love. The more time you can spend with your child, the more influence you will have over his or her healthy development.

Bedtime can be an especially good time to bond with your child. During the child's infancy, try to be there to put him or her in the crib at night. As the child grows older, read bedtime stories to him or her. Children enjoy listening to a story, looking at the pictures, pointing to pages in the book, and asking questions. Most important, they appreciate the fact that Dad is reading the story to them.

As a father, the days that you spend with your small child are only the beginning. The joys and challenges will continue as your child grows older. And the decision that you made to become a teen father will have a profound impact on the rest of your life.

Glossary

abortion Termination of a pregnancy prior to birth.

absentee father A father who is not present to help care for his child.

acknowledgement of paternity A form that establishes the father of a child.

anxiety Fear or feeling of uneasiness.

baby blues Sadness or emotional discomfort that a woman feels after delivery.

compromise A basic negotiation process by which both parties give up something in order to arrive at a greater agreement.

daycare Child care while the parents are at work or, in the case of many teen parents, in school.

fetus An unborn child.

hormones Chemicals released in the endocrine system that affect various organs in the body.

morning sickness Nausea and vomiting experienced by a woman during the early months of pregnancy, usually in the morning.

obligation Duty or responsibility; something that one is bound to do.

paternity Being a father.

postpartum depression Feelings of depression a woman experiences after delivery.

prenatal care Health care a woman receives during pregnancy.

priority Something requiring or meriting attention before other things.

role model Person worthy of imitation; individual after whom one models his or her behavior.

tantrum Emotional outburst or fit of bad temper that is common in young children.

trimester A three-month period during pregnancy; there are three trimesters in a pregnancy.

uterus Female organ in which a fetus grows.

For More Information

American Pregnancy Association
1431 Greenway Drive, Suite 800
Irving, TX 75038
(972) 550-0140
Web site: http://www.americanpregnancy.org

The American Pregnancy Association focuses on helping parents understand their pregnancy.

Child Development Institute
1442 E. Lincoln Avenue, #419
Orange, CA 92865
(866) 510-6556
Web site: http://www.childdevelopmentinfo.com

This organization offers parents information on family life, learning, health and safety, child psychology, and the stages of child development.

Head Start
Administration for Children and Families (ACF)
370 L'Enfant Promenade SW
Washington, DC 20201
Web site: http://www.acf.hhs.gov

Part of the ACF, Head Start is a preschool program that was established by the federal government. It's primarily

aimed at helping low-income parents who may be unable to afford a preschool program.

National Association of Child Care Resource and Referral Agencies (NACCRRA)
3101 Wilson Boulevard, Suite 350
Arlington, VA 22201
(703) 341-4100
Web site: http://www.naccrra.org

NACCRRA is the leading voice for child care in the United States. The organization provides training and resources to more than eight hundred state and local Child Care Resource and Referral agencies worldwide.

National Center for Fathering
P.O. Box 413888
Kansas City, MO 64141
(800) 593-DADS (3237)
Web site: http://www.fathers.com

This educational organization provides practical, research-based training and resources that help fathers in virtually every parenting situation.

National Child Care Information Center
10530 Rosehaven Street, Suite 400
Fairfax, VA 22030
(800) 616-2242
Web site: http://www.nccic.org

Part of the ACF, the National Child Care Information Center promotes good parenting by providing advice for successful child rearing.

National Fatherhood Initiative
One Bank Street, Suite 160
Gaithersburg, MD 20878
(301) 948-0599
Web site: http://www.fatherhood.org

This organization seeks to encourage young fathers to invest the time, commitment, and responsibility necessary for good fathering.

Web Sites

Due to the changing nature of Internet links, Rosen Publishing has developed an online list of Web sites related to the subject of this book. This site is updated regularly. Please use this link to access the list:

http://www.rosenlinks.com/faq/fath

For Further Reading

Frick, Lisa, ed. *Teenage Pregnancy and Parenting*. San Diego, CA: Greenhaven Press, 2007.

Gottfried, Ted. *Teen Fathers Today*. Breckenridge, CO: Twenty-First Century Books, 2001.

Lindsay, Jeanne Warren. *Teen Dads: Rights, Responsibilities, and Joys*. Buena Park, CO: Morning Glory Press, 2001.

Lindsay, Jeanne Warren. *Your Pregnancy and Newborn Journey: A Guide for Pregnant Teens*. Buena Park, CO: Morning Glory Press, 2004.

Nolan, Mary. *Teen Pregnancy*. New York, NY: Heinemann Library, 2003.

Ojeda, Auriana, ed. *Teenage Pregnancy: Opposing Viewpoints*. San Diego, CA: Greenhaven Press, 2003.

Index

N

O

P

R

S

T

U

About the Author

Richard Worth is an award-winning author who has written more than fifty books for young adults, some of them on family living. This is his first book for Rosen Publishing.

Photo Credits

Cover © www.istockphoto.com/Justin Horrocks; pp. 5, 50 © David Young-Wolff/Photo Edit; p. 7 © Todd Williamson/ WireImage for Elizabeth Glaser; p. 8 © www.istockphoto.com/ Liv Frtis-Larsen; p. 11 © www.istockphoto.com/Tamara Gentuso; p. 13 © www.istockphoto.com/Elena Korenbaum; p. 17 © Nancy Sheehan/Photo Edit; p. 20 © www.istockphoto.com/ Jonathan Nourok; p. 25 © John Birdsall/Image Works; p. 28 © Shutterstock; p. 30 © www.istockphoto.com; p. 34 © www. istockphoto.com/Vicki Reid; p. 37 © www.istockphoto.com/ Jacom Stephens; p. 38 © www.istockphoto.com/Joris van Caspel; p. 42 © www.istockphoto.com/Diane Diederich; p. 49 © Janet Jarman/Corbis; p. 53 © www.istockphoto.com/Annett Vauteck; p. 54 © Mary Kate Denny/Photo Edit.

Designer: Nicole Russo; Editor: Christopher Roberts;
Photo Researcher: Marty Levick

S0-BRG-928